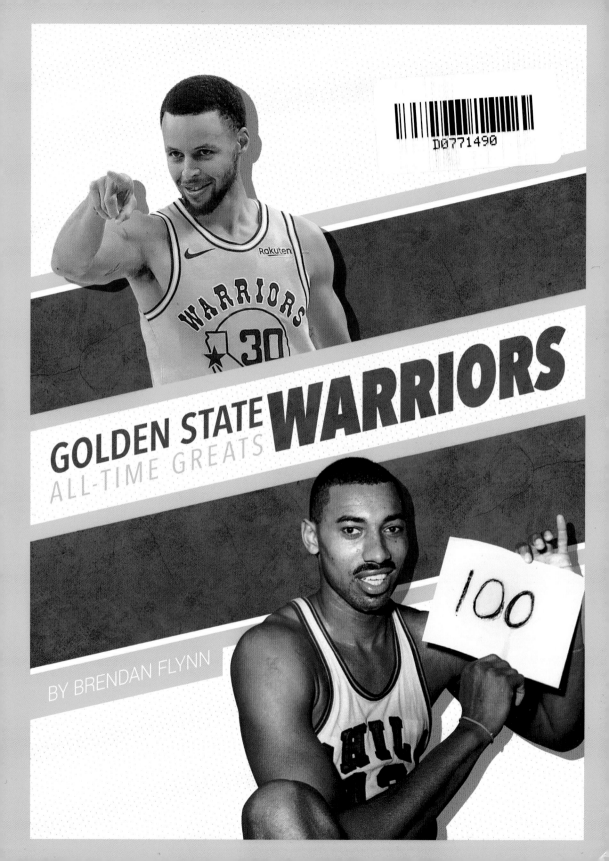

GOLDEN STATE WARRIORS
ALL-TIME GREATS

BY BRENDAN FLYNN

Book design by Jake Slavik
Cover design by Jake Slavik

Photographs ©: Jeff Chiu/AP Images, cover (top), 1 (top); Paul Vathis/AP Images, cover (bottom), 1 (bottom), 4; Bettmann/Getty Images, 7, 8; George Long/Sports Illustrated/ Set Number: X17597 TK3/Getty Images, 10; Focus on Sport/Getty Images, 11; Tim DeFrisco/ Sports Illustrated/Set Number: X42102/Getty Images, 12; Peter Read Miller/Sports Illustrated/ Set Number: X42099/Getty Images, 14; Ezra Shaw/Getty Images Sport/Getty Images, 16; Marcio Jose Sanchez/AP Images, 19; Greg Nelson/Sports Illustrated/Set Number: X161965 TK1/Getty Images, 20; Red Line Editorial, 22

Press Box Books, an imprint of Press Room Editions.

ISBN
978-1-63494-153-2 (library bound)
978-1-63494-166-2 (paperback)
978-1-63494-179-2 (epub)
978-1-63494-192-1 (hosted ebook)

Library of Congress Control Number: 2019951049

Distributed by North Star Editions, Inc.
2297 Waters Drive
Mendota Heights, MN 55120
www.northstareditions.com

Printed in the United States of America
012020

ABOUT THE AUTHOR

Brendan Flynn is a San Francisco resident and an author of numerous children's books. In addition to writing about sports, Flynn also enjoys competing in triathlons, Scrabble tournaments, and chili cook-offs.

TABLE OF CONTENTS

CHAMBERLAIN
13

CHAPTER 1
OLD SCHOOL

The Golden State Warriors are one of the NBA's oldest teams. However, they haven't always played in California. They started out in Philadelphia. The Warriors were founded in 1946, three years before the NBA was formed. They even won a title in their first year of existence.

The Warriors spent 16 years in Philadelphia. The great **Wilt Chamberlain** became a star in a Philadelphia Warriors uniform. By the early 1960s, the West Coast was becoming a hotbed for professional sports. The Warriors followed the trend and moved to San Francisco in 1962. But they formed a lot of memories with a lot of great players in Philadelphia.

Their first superstar was hometown hero **Paul Arizin**. The Philadelphia native changed the game when he joined the Warriors as a rookie in 1950. Arizin was one of the first to use the jump shot as a weapon. An athletic small forward, he led the league in scoring twice. Arizin missed two seasons due to military service. But he was still an All-Star in each of his 10 NBA seasons, all spent in Philadelphia.

Center **Neil Johnston** came on board in Arizin's second year. He used a deadly hook shot to lead the league in scoring three years in a row.

ARIZIN
11

CHAMBERLAIN
13

Johnston and Arizin combined to lead
the Warriors to the NBA title in 1956. They
wouldn't win another in Philadelphia, but the
team still had some huge moments. One came

on March 2, 1962. That night, third-year center Chamberlain scored 100 points in a game. That shattered his own NBA record. No player has come within 19 points of matching it since.

The 7'1" superstar dominated the NBA like few have ever done. He led the league in scoring in each of his first seven seasons. That included an all-time record of 50.4 points per game in 1961–62. Chamberlain spent nearly six years with the Warriors. The first three were in his native Philadelphia. Midway through his third season in California, he was traded back to his hometown's new team, the 76ers.

THURMOND
42

Two more Hall of Famers started out with the Warriors in San Francisco. **Nate Thurmond** was a defensive force who also had a nice touch on his jump shot. At 6'11", he ruled the lane long before blocked shots were an official statistic. The seven-time All-Star spent 11 seasons with the Warriors. He retired as the team's all-time leading rebounder.

Meanwhile, flashy forward **Rick Barry** took the league by storm in 1965. In his second season, Barry scored a league-high 35.6 points per game. He then played four years in the American Basketball Association. But he returned to lead the Warriors to the 1975 NBA title.

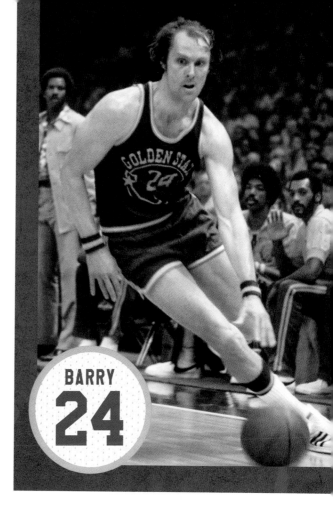

BARRY
24

MOST CAREER REBOUNDS
WARRIORS TEAM RECORD
Nate Thurmond: 12,771

MULLIN
17

CHAPTER 2
BAY AREA REVIVAL

The Warriors went through some lean years after winning the 1975 championship. But in 1988, head coach **Don Nelson** arrived. He installed a fast-paced offense. Not only were the Warriors fun to watch, they were also pretty good. Nelson guided the team to the playoffs in his first year. They returned three more times in the next five seasons.

Small forward **Chris Mullin** was the star of those teams. In his first five seasons under Nelson he scored an average of 25.8 points per game. He was an All-Star in each of those seasons.

HARDAWAY
10

Mullin was a member of the US "Dream Team" that cruised to Olympic gold in 1992. But back in the Bay Area, he was part of "Run-TMC," the highest-scoring trio in the league.

Run-TMC also included shooting guard **Mitch Richmond** and point guard **Tim Hardaway**. They teamed up to make Nelson's offense hum.

Hardaway in particular thrived. He averaged 22.7 points and 10.0 assists per game over a three-year span starting in 1990. Richmond was a prolific scorer with a deadly jumper. The team peaked with an upset of the Spurs in the first round of the 1991 playoffs, followed by a 55-win season.

STAT SPOTLIGHT

MOST CAREER STEALS
WARRIORS TEAM RECORD
Chris Mullin: 1,360

CHAPTER 3
CHAMPIONS

Another dry spell soon followed. Golden State made the playoffs just once in 18 seasons. But smart drafting and savvy coaching would help the Warriors become the NBA's top franchise. Beginning in 2014-15, they reached five straight NBA Finals, winning three. They also set the NBA regular-season record with 73 wins in 2015-16.

A number of players became household names during that run. One of them was a scrawny kid from a tiny college who made himself into one of the best shooters in NBA history—**Steph Curry**.

Curry's father, Dell, was an NBA sharpshooter himself. But Steph surpassed his dad, earning a reputation as a player who might shoot from anywhere on the floor. Curry began raining three-pointers on opponents' heads at a furious pace. He made the most three-pointers in the NBA five years in a row.

Curry and backcourt mate **Klay Thompson** became known as "the Splash Brothers" for their long-distance shooting. Curry won back-to-back NBA Most Valuable Player (MVP) Awards. Thompson wasn't far behind him. He averaged more than 20 points per game in five straight All-Star seasons.

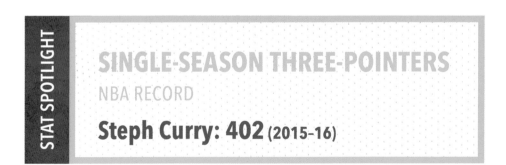

STAT SPOTLIGHT

SINGLE-SEASON THREE-POINTERS
NBA RECORD
Steph Curry: 402 (2015-16)

THOMPSON
11

GREEN
23

Those championship teams relied on forward **Draymond Green** to contribute a little bit of everything. A gifted passer, Green averaged 7.1 assists per game over a four-year stretch. He also played tenacious defense. He often guarded the opponent's top player. That included head-to-head battles with LeBron James in four consecutive NBA Finals. Green and the Warriors won three of them.

The team added another weapon in former league MVP **Kevin Durant** in 2016. Durant averaged nearly 30 points per game in the playoffs and won two NBA Finals MVP Awards in the next three seasons.

BACK TO SAN FRANCISCO

After spending 47 seasons playing their home games in Oakland, the Warriors moved across the bay. They opened Chase Center in downtown San Francisco to start the 2019–20 season.

TIMELINE

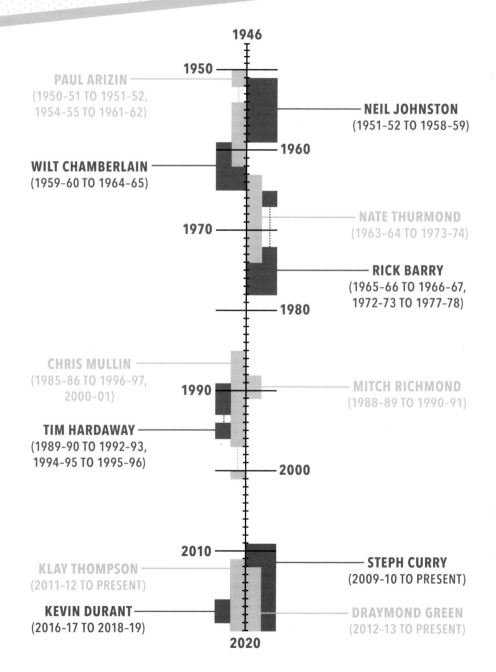

1946

1950

PAUL ARIZIN
(1950-51 TO 1951-52,
1954-55 TO 1961-62)

NEIL JOHNSTON
(1951-52 TO 1958-59)

1960

WILT CHAMBERLAIN
(1959-60 TO 1964-65)

NATE THURMOND
(1963-64 TO 1973-74)

1970

RICK BARRY
(1965-66 TO 1966-67,
1972-73 TO 1977-78)

1980

CHRIS MULLIN
(1985-86 TO 1996-97,
2000-01)

MITCH RICHMOND
(1988-89 TO 1990-91)

1990

TIM HARDAWAY
(1989-90 TO 1992-93,
1994-95 TO 1995-96)

2000

2010

KLAY THOMPSON
(2011-12 TO PRESENT)

STEPH CURRY
(2009-10 TO PRESENT)

KEVIN DURANT
(2016-17 TO 2018-19)

DRAYMOND GREEN
(2012-13 TO PRESENT)

2020

TEAM FACTS

GOLDEN STATE WARRIORS

Formerly: Philadelphia Warriors (1946–47 to 1961–62); San Francisco Warriors (1962–63 to 1970–71)

First season: 1946–47

NBA championships: 6*

Key coaches:

Al Attles (1969–70 to 1982–83)
557–518, 31–30 playoffs, 1 NBA title

Edward Gottleib (1946–47 to 1954–55)
263–318, 15–17 playoffs, 1 NBA title

Steve Kerr (2014–15 to present)
322–88, 77–28 playoffs, 3 NBA titles

MORE INFORMATION

To learn more about the Golden State Warriors, go to **pressboxbooks.com/AllAccess**.

These links are routinely monitored and updated to provide the most current information available.

Through 2018–19 season

GLOSSARY

deadly
Consistently accurate.

founded
Established or formed.

hook shot
A one-handed shot in which a player extends one arm out to the side and over the head toward the basket.

lane
The area directly between the free-throw line and the basket.

prolific
Productive or plentiful.

rookie
A first-year player.

savvy
Clever or intelligent.

scrawny
Skinny, underfed.

tenacious
Hard-working, difficult to shake off.

thrived
Was successful.

trio
A group of three.

INDEX